CELIUS DOUGHERTY

FOLKSONGS AND CHANTIES

LOW VOICE AND PIANO

ED 8196

ISBN 0-634-07333-8

G. SCHIRMER, Inc.

DISTRIBUTED BY

HAL•LEONARD®
CORPORATION
7777 W. BLUEMOUND RD. P.O. BOX 13819 MILWAUKEE, WI 53213

www.schirmer.com
www.halleonard.com

Celius Dougherty
1902-1986

American composer, accompanist and duo-pianist, Celius Dougherty was born in Glenwood, Minnesota, into a family so musical that his music teacher/church choirmaster mother organized her seven children into a band. His first public performance, at age ten, was as accompanist for one of his mother's song recitals. After graduating from the University of Minnesota, he moved to New York to study piano and composition at Juilliard. He soon became a sought-after recital accompanist, touring Europe and making RCA records with the great Russian baritone, Alexander Kipnis, Canada's adventurous Eva Gauthier, and Sweden's Povla Frijsch, whom he admired for her interpretive abilities.

In 1939 Dougherty formed a two-piano team with Vincenz Ruzicka, appearing in every U.S. state and in Vienna with the Vienna Symphony in 1955. The duo was noted for giving world premieres of important new works for two pianos: Hindemith's *Sonata for Two Pianos*, Stravinsky's *Sonata for Two Pianos*, Berg's *Suite from Lulu*, Schönberg's *Variations on a Recitative*. Some of these were works for orchestra, which he arranged for two pianos. Another was a sonata, which he arranged from nautical themes, *Music from Seas and Ships,* dedicated to his brother Ralph, who went down with the U.S.S. Arizona at Pearl Harbor.

Dougherty's catalogue of compositions includes a one-act opera for children, *Many Moons*, based on a story by James Thurber, as well as a piano concerto, a string quartet, and sonatas for violin, piano, and piano duo. But he is best remembered for 200 gracious and witty songs. His early songs were settings of English and American poets: Walt Whitman, e.e. cummings, Amy Lowell, Robert Frost and Siegfried Sassoon. Later songs derived from essays by children, Chinese poetry, the dictionary, newspapers, spirituals and folksongs.

Further information on this publication, the availability of other works, performances and more background on the composer can be found at www.celiusdougherty.org.

FOLKSONG ARRANGEMENTS

FIVE SEA CHANTIES

BARBARA ALLEN

original key: F-sharp Major

Scottish Folksong
Arranged by
Celius Dougherty

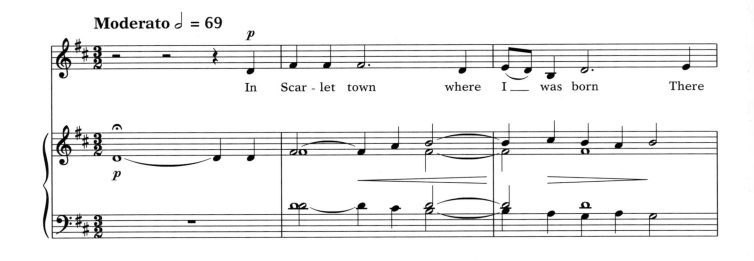

In Scar - let town where I __ was born   There

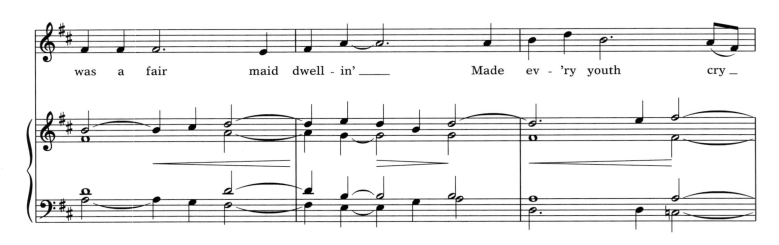

was a fair   maid dwell - in' ___   Made ev - 'ry youth   cry __

well a - way   Her __ name was Bar - b'ra Al - len.

One day, one day, in the month of May When green buds were a-swell-in' Young Jem-my Grove on his death-bed lay For love of Bar-b'ra Al-len. He sent his man un-to her then, To the

town where she was dwell-in' ___ "O haste and come to my

master dear, If your name be Bar - b'ra Al - len." ___

So slow-ly, slow - ly rose ___ she up, And

slow - ly came she to him, ___ And when she drew the ___

cur - tain by: "Young man, I think you're dy - in'." _

"O I am sick and ve - ry, ve - ry sick, And it's

all for Bar - b'ra Al - len." _ "O it's bet - ter for me ye's _

nev - er be, Though your heart's blood be a - spill - in'." _

"O din-na ye mind, young man," said she, "When the

red wine ye were fill-in', ____ Ye made the healths go ____

round and round, And slight-ed Bar-b'ra Al-len." ____

He turned his face un-to ____ the wall For

death was with him deal - in' ___ "A - dieu, a - dieu, my ___

ancòre più **p**

dear friends all, Be kind to Bar - b'ra Al - len." ___

rit.

pp

p *a tempo*

As she was walk - in' o'er ___ the fields, She

heard the death - bell knell - in' ___ And ev - 'ry toll the ___

"Fare - well," she said, "ye virgins all, And shun the fault I fell in; ___ Hence - forth take warn - ing _ by the fate Of cru - el Bar - b'ra Al - len." __

poco allargando

BUFFALO BOY

original key

American Folksong
Arranged by
Celius Dougherty

O when are you com-in' to court me, to court me, to court me, O when are you com-in' to court me, my dear old Buf-fa-lo Boy? I guess I'll come on Sun - day, on Sun - day, on

wed - din', _ to the wed - din', _ to the wed - din', _ Well

who you gon - na bring to the wed - din', _ my dear old Buf - fa - lo

Boy? I guess I'll bring my chil - dren, my chil - dren, my

chil - dren, I guess I'll bring my chil - dren, That is if the weath - er is

chil - dren, May-be six if the weath-er is good. Well, there ain't goin' to be no

wed - din', no wed - din', no wed - din', Well, there ain't goin' to be no

wed - din', Not e - ven if the weath-er is good!

BRING MY LULU HOME

original key

From *American Ballads and Folksongs*
Collected by John and Alan Lomax★

American Folksong
Arranged by
Celius Dougherty

★Words and melody used by permission of Mrs. John A. Lomax

COLORADO TRAIL

original key

American Folksong
Arranged by
Celius Dougherty

Eyes like the morn-ing star, Cheek like a rose,

Sal - ly was a pret-ty gal, God Al-might-y knows. Weep, all ye lit-tle rains,

Wail, winds, wail, All a-long, a-long, a-long the Col - o-ra-do Trail.

Sweet as the li-lac grows,

Fair in the sun, Sal - ly was a pret-ty gal, God Al-might-y knows.

Weep, all ye lit-tle rains, Wail, winds, wail, All a-long, a-long, a-long the

Col - o - ra - do Trail, A-long the

Col - o - ra - do Trail.

COME ALL YOU FAIR AND TENDER MAIDENS

original key: F Major

American Folksong from Kentucky
Arranged by
Celius Dougherty

Come all you fair and ten-der maid-ens, Be care-ful how you court young men, They're like a star of a sum-mer's morn-ing, They first ap-pear and then they're gone.

Do you re - mem - ber on yon - der _ moun - tain, Where you and I first fell in _ love? The _ lit - tle birds were _ sing - ing _ sweet - ly And may - be too the _ lit - tle _ doves. _ If I had know'd be - fore I _ court - ed That love had

been so hard to __ win, I'd __ lock'd my heart in a box of __

gold - en And pinned it down with a sil - ver __ pin. ____

Men al - ways tell some __ pleas - ing __

sto - ry And then de - clare they are your __ own, Straight - way they'll

I WISH I WERE ON YONDER HILL

original key

American Revolutionary Song
Adapted from "Sìul a Ruin"
Arranged by
Celius Dougherty

Andante non troppo

wish I were on yon-der hill, 'Tis there I'd sit and cry my fill Till

ev-'ry tear would turn a mill *Iss goh teh____ too moh - voor__ neen__

*This is the phonetic spelling of a Gaelic phrase meaning, "A blessing walk with you my love."

THE LADY WHO LOVED A PIG

original key

American Folksong
Arranged by
Celius Dougherty

From **Our Singing Country**
Collected by John and Alan Lomax★

★ Words and melody used by permission of Mrs. John A. Lomax.

★★ optional falsetto if sung by a male singer

he. "I'll build for thee a

sil - ver sty, Hon - ey,"＿＿＿ said she,

"And in it thou shalt lie." "Humph," said

★★ optional falsetto

he. "I'll pin it with a sil - ver pin,

Hon - ey," said she, "That thou mayst go out and in."

"Humph," said he.

★★ optional falsetto

"O wilt thou have me now," said she, "Hon - ey,"_____ said

she, "Speak, or my heart will break."

"Humph," said he.

★★ optional falsetto

O WALY, WALY

original key: A Major

English Folksong
Arranged by
Celius Dougherty

Moderato con mosso

The wa-ter is wide, I can-not get o'er, And nei-ther

have I wings to __ fly, Give me a __ boat that will car-ry __

two, And both shall row, my love and __ I.

O down in the mea - dow the o - ther day A - gath - 'ring

flow'rs both fine and _ gay, A - gath - 'ring _ flow'rs both red and _

blue I lit - tle thought what love can _ do.

I laid my breast up a-gainst an oak, Think-ing that

RED RIVER VALLEY

original key: G Major

19th Century American Folksong
Arranged by
Celius Dougherty

mp *poco più mosso*

while. _____ Will you think of the val - ley you're

cantando — **mp**

leav - ing, _ Oh, how lone - ly and sad it will be? Will you

think of the Red Riv - er Val - ley _ And the grief you are caus - ing to

o - cean, _ May you nev - er for - get the sweet hours That we

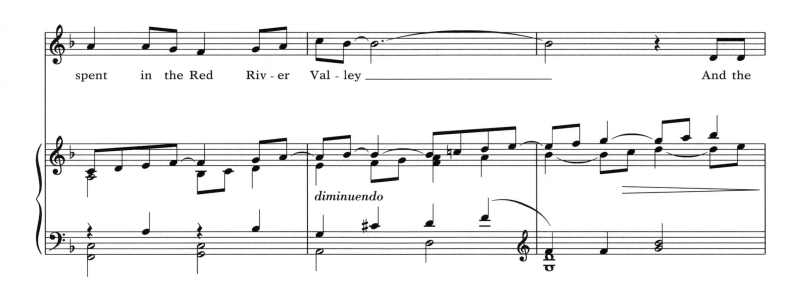

spent in the Red Riv - er Val - ley _____ And the

rit. molto **Lento**

sweet - heart that's wait - ing for you. _____

SHADY GROVE

original key: G minor

American Folksong
Arranged by
Celius Dougherty

Shady grove, my true love,
Shady grove I know,
Shady grove, my true love, I'm

Sha - dy grove, my true love, Sha - dy grove I know,

Sha - dy grove, my __ true __ love, I'm bound for the sha - dy

grove. _____

with pedal

no pedal

STEWBALL

original key: C Major

From **American Ballads and Folksongs**
Collected by John and Alan Lomax ★

American Folksong
Arranged by
Celius Dougherty

★ Words and melody used by permission of Mrs. John A. Lomax

storm, a storm, in a storm, man, in a storm. _____ Ol'

Stew - ball _ was a white horse be - fore they, _ 'fore they

paint him red, But he sure winned _ a great for-tune jes' be -

fore he _ fell dead, fell dead, fell dead, man, fell

bang-in' fo' the hors-es to _ run, to run, And ol'

Stew-ball was a - trem-blin' like a crim-i-nal to be

hung, to be hung, to be hung, man, to be hung. _____ But you

should've seen ol' _ Stew-ball, _ how he ram-bled _ down that

WAYFARING STRANGER

original key: E-flat minor

American Folksong from the South
Arranged by
Celius Dougherty

Andante

I'm just a poor way-far-ing stran-ger A-wan-d'ring through this vale of woe. But there's no sor - row, toil, nor dan-ger In that far land to which I go. I'm go-ing

* Editor's note: All -ing endings might be sung as -in' throughout for appropriate style.

saints their vi-gils keep. I'm go-ing there to meet my moth-er, I'm go-ing

there no more to roam. I'm just a - go - ing o - ver Jor-dan, I'm just a -

go - ing o - ver home. I'm just a poor way-far-ing

stran - ger a-trav'-ling through this world of woe. But there's no

WHAT YOU GONNA DO WHEN THE MEAT GIVES OUT?

American Folksong
Arranged by
Celius Dougherty

original key: F Major

I'll be blamed if I can see

How all my mon-ey got a-way from me,— for

some time.—

What kind of pants does the gam-bler wear,— my ba—by?

FIVE SEA CHANTIES

RIO GRANDE

original key: E-flat Major

American Sea Chanty
Arranged by
Celius Dougherty

Oh! _ say, was you ev - er in Ri - o Grande? Oh, _____ you Ri - o! _____ Oh, _ say, was you ev - er on __ that strand? Oh, _____ you Ri -

o! _____ Our ship is a - go - ing out o - ver the bar, For we're

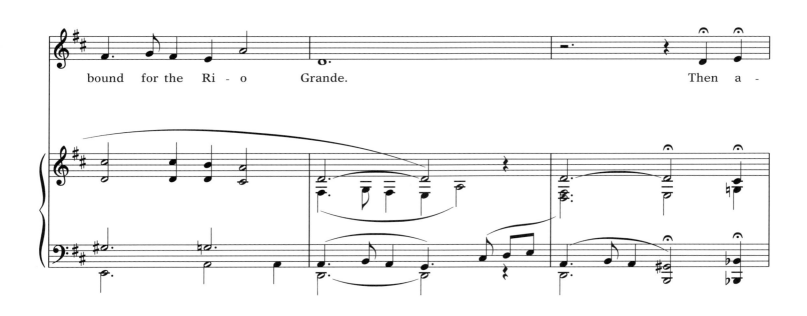

bound for the Ri - o Grande. Then a -

way, _____ you Ri - o, 'Way, _____ you Ri -

o, _____ We'll point her nose for the South-er-on star, For we're

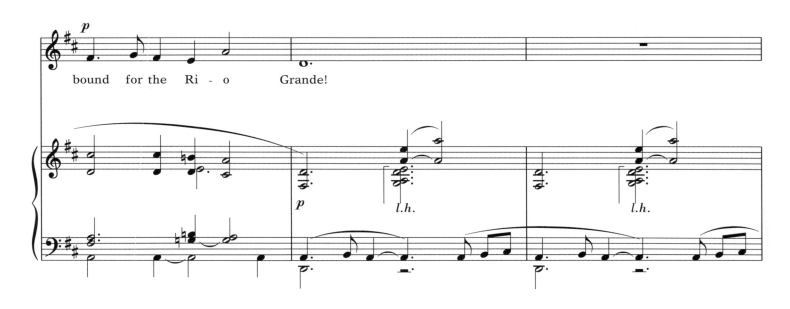

bound for the Ri - o Grande!

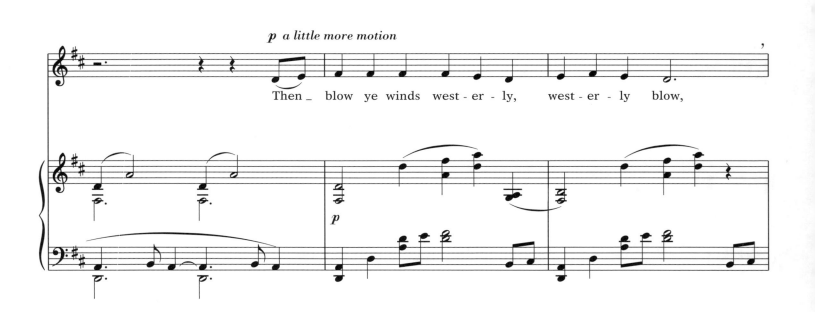

p a little more motion

Then _ blow ye winds west-er - ly, west-er - ly blow,

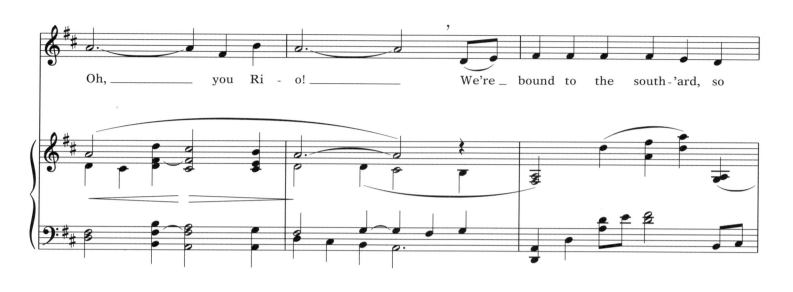

Oh, _____ you Ri - o! _____ We're _ bound to the south-'ard, so

stead - y she goes, Oh, _____ you Ri - o! _____ Sing

good - bye to Nel - lie, sing good - bye to Sue, For we're bound for the Ri - o

Grande.   Then a - way, _____ you Ri -

o,   'Way, _____ you Ri - o, _____ And

you who are lis - ten - ing, good - bye to you, For we're bound for the Ri - o

Grande.

f And you who are lis - ten - ing,

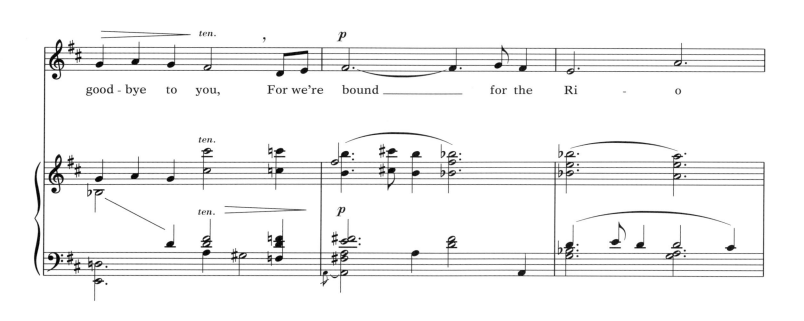

good - bye to you, For we're bound _____ for the Ri - o

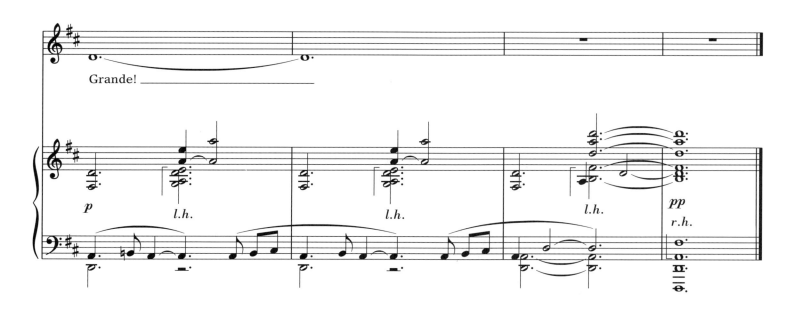

Grande!

BLOW, YE WINDS

original key

18th Century American Sea Chanty
Arranged by
Celius Dougherty

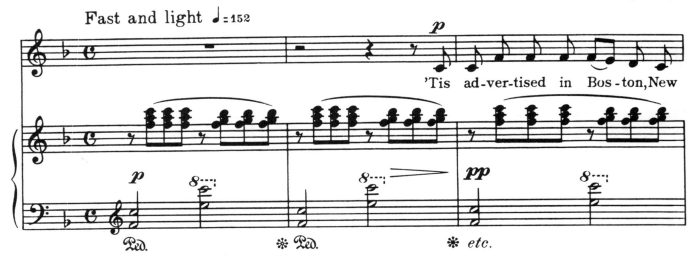

blow, ye winds, heigh - o. Clear a-way your run-ning gear and

blow, ye winds, heigh - o. They

send you to New Bed - ford, that fa - mous whal - ing port. They

put you on a clip - per ship be - fore you know you're out,— sing - ing,

Blow, ye winds in the morn - ing, blow, ye winds, heigh - o.

Clear a-way your run-ning gear and blow, ye winds, heigh - o.

It's now we're out to sea, boys, the wind comes on to blow. One

But now our trip is o - ver and we don't give a damn. We'll

bend on all our stu'n - sails and sail for Yan - kee land, sing - ing,

Blow, ye winds in the morn - ing, blow, ye winds, heigh - o.

Clear a-way your run-ning gear and blow, ye winds, heigh - o.

Blow, ye winds in the morn-ing,

soft but clear

in tempo

blow, ye winds, heigh-o.

in memory of my brother Ralph

ACROSS THE WESTERN OCEAN

original key

Irish Sea Chanty
Arranged by
Celius Dougherty

84

MOBILE BAY

African-American Chanty
Arranged by
Celius Dougherty

original key

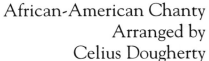

Johnny, come tell us and heave a-way. Aye, aye, heave a-way,

Heave a-way, and draw your pay. A dol-lar a day is a sail-or's pay, To

work all night and pump all day. The

work is hard, the ship is old, John-ny, come tell us and heave a-way, There's

six feet of wa-ter in her hold; John-ny, come tell us and heave a-way.

Aye, aye,— heave a-way, Heave a-way and draw your pay, The

draw your pay, The rats have gone, and we, the crew, It's

time, by God, that we went

too!

SHENANDOAH

original key

American Sea Chanty
Arranged by
Celius Dougherty

'Cross the wide Mis - sou - ri. Mis -

sou - ri she's__ a might - y riv - er, Hi - o! you roll - ing

riv - er, When she rolls down__ her top-sails shiv - er, Hi -